ARCHIMEDES

INNOVATIVE MATHEMATICIAN, ENGINEER, AND INVENTOR

THE GREATEST GREEK PHILOSOPHERS

ARCHIMEDES

INNOVATIVE MATHEMATICIAN, ENGINEER, AND INVENTOR

VIOLA JONES & HEATHER HASAN

ROSEN PUBLISHING

NEW YORK

Published in 2016 by The Rosen Publishing Group, Inc.
29 East 21st Street, New York, NY 10010

Copyright © 2016 by The Rosen Publishing Group, Inc.

First Edition

Library of Congress Cataloging-in-Publication Data

Jones, Viola, author.
Archimedes: innovative mathematician, engineer, and inventor/Viola Jones and Heather Hasan.
pages cm.—(The greatest Greek philosophers)
Includes bibliographical references and index.
ISBN 978-1-4994-6124-4 (library bound)
1. Archimedes—Juvenile literature. 2. Mathematicians—Greece—Biography—Juvenile literature. 3. Philosophers—Greece—Biography—Juvenile literature. I. Hasan, Heather, author. II. Title.
QA29.A7J66 2015
510.92—dc23
[B]

2014045856

Manufactured in the United States of America

CONTENTS

K nown as "the Father of Mathematics," Archimedes was the most important mathematician and inventor in ancient Greece. His brilliant mind is responsible for many contributions to both theoretical and applied mathematics. Thanks to their close friendship, Archimedes was called upon by the king to solve many royal problems. His solutions resulted in many inventions and innovations that are still in use today.

Archimedes was born around 287 BCE in Syracuse, a city situated on the eastern coast of the island of Sicily, in the Mediterranean Sea. Though Syracuse is now part of Italy, it was part of Greece at the time of Archimedes's birth. The first people recorded to have lived in Sicily were the Sicans. These people inhabited the island by 10,000 BCE. The Sicans were driven from the island by the Sicels, who gave the island its name. Because of Sicily's good geographical position for trade and the fertility of its soil, the island attracted many navigators. Among them were the Phoenicians, who originated from the coast of North Africa, and the Greeks.

Around 733 BCE, Greek colonists from Corinth (in southern Greece) built the city of Syracuse, driving the native Sicels from that area. From there, Syracuse grew rapidly. The Corinthian Greeks moved westward, and, in 691 BCE, they also settled Gela, an area on the southwestern coast of the island. By 635 BCE, the Greeks had successfully driven the Phoenicians to the western part

The most famous mathematician and inventor in all of ancient Greece was Archimedes, who is often called the Father of Mathematics.

of the island, an area near what is known today as Palermo. Eventually, Sicily became home to more Greeks than Greece itself.

Under the rule of the Greeks, Sicily soon became highly civilized and prosperous. This prosperity was the result of trade, both by land and sea. Syracuse entered the fifth century BCE as the strongest and most important of all the Greek cities of Sicily. However, Syracuse's vast wealth and resources invited conquest, and, for years, the people of Syracuse had to fight off raids.

During this time, Syracuse also faced repeated conflicts with the Phoenicians who had settled in the western part of Sicily. Ever since their arrival in western Sicily, the Phoenicians had intermarried with the native people of that area. Over the years, they had become known as the Carthaginians or the Punics. The word "Punic" comes from the Greek word *phoinikos*, which means "purple" and probably

Sicily became a highly desirable city vulnerable to attack. This map shows the western Mediterranean during the Punic Wars, fought between Rome and Carthage.

referred to the purple dye that was produced in the area. The Syracusans and the Carthaginians fought constantly to expel each other from Sicily.

For centuries, Syracuse swung back and forth between a democracy and a dictatorship. The idea of democracy, government ruled by the people, was first introduced to the world by the Greeks. Their ideas of democracy, trial by jury, and equality under the law formed the foundation on which Western civilization was built. However, in between the times of democracy were times of dictatorship, where the people were ruled by the decisions of one man. The men who rose to power during the times of dictatorship were known as tyrants, though the word "tyrant" in Greek does not carry as negative a meaning as it does in English. These rulers were called tyrants because they took rule by force.

In the late third century BCE, a group of Italian mercenaries, who had been hired by the Greeks, seized Messana (modern-day Messina), a town strategically located on the straights separating Sicily from Italy. These mercenaries, or hired soldiers, called themselves Mamertines. They used the town of Messana as a base for raiding other nearby towns, and Syracuse was located dangerously close. In 269 BCE, a new tyrant, King Hiero II, emerged in Syracuse. He ruled from 269 to 215 BCE (much of Archimedes's adult life). Hiero attacked the Mamertines in order to protect Syracuse. The Mamertines, in turn, appealed to Rome for assistance.

At that time, the Romans controlled much of what is now Italy. The Carthaginians, not wanting the

Romans to intervene in Sicily, sent naval and ground forces to Messana. The Mamertines accepted help from Carthage, forcing King Hiero to withdraw. After some time, however, the requested Roman forces also arrived in Messana. When the armies from Rome and Carthage met, war erupted. This marked the beginning of the first of the three wars fought between the Romans and the Carthaginians, called the Punic Wars. These long and exhausting conflicts greatly affected both Archimedes's life and his work.

During the First Punic War (264–241 BCE), Syracuse initially supported Carthage. However, early in the war, Rome forced a treaty of alliance from King Hiero. At the end of the war, the Carthaginians and the Romans signed a treaty in which Carthage gave up Sicily. Rome made the rest of Sicily a province but left Syracuse as an independent Greek city. It was in this atmosphere that Archimedes lived out most of his life.

The time period into which Archimedes was born has come to be known as the Hellenistic period (323–30 BCE). The word "Hellenistic" is derived from *Hellenes*, which is simply the Greek word for "Greek." The Hellenistic period began with the death of Alexander the Great in 323 BCE and ended with Rome's occupation of the last major Hellenistic kingdom in approximately 30 BCE. The Hellenistic period was marked by the spread of Greek ideas and culture. A Greek dialect became a common one and was the language used for trade and commerce. The Greeks tended to view anyone who spoke their language and shared in their customs as part of their culture. The

Greeks had a great influence on the people of their time, and this influence continues even into modern times. They shaped our laws, our arts, and our sciences. They also

Archimedes invented the "iron hand" for King Hiero. This device lifted attacking ships out of the water. It is known as the Claw of Archimedes.

laid the foundation for our ethical standards, how we view right and wrong.

The Hellenistic period was a time when most things flourished, including the arts and the economy. Hellenistic art, mostly sculptures, have survived to this day. Painting was important also, but not much remains besides copies made by the Romans. The Hellenistic period was a time of naturalistic art. The art was very expressive, often showing violently constricted bodies displaying great emotion. Much of the literature that existed during the Hellenistic period was poetry. The Greeks developed tragedy, comedy, and lyric (song-like) poetry. Theocritus of Syracuse was known for his writing of pastoral idyll and bucolic poems—short, descriptive poems about country life. Many of his poems survive today.

A number of philosophies existed during the Hellenistic period. Many Hellenistic people practiced a philosophy called humanism. Also known as man-worship, humanism focuses on the needs and interests of people. Many philosophers of the time focused on achieving peace of mind. The Epicurean philosophers believed that it is best to have a little pleasure and very little pain. Another philosophy, called Stoicism, held the idea that a divine mind controlled the world and planned the course of people's lives. Stoics believed that happiness resulted when people grasped this idea and simply tried to live their already planned lives as best they could. The Cynics, who practiced a philosophy called Cynicism, tried to disregard all pleasures and desires, seeking only to live virtuously.

The Hellenistic period is also known for its advances in science. Great discoveries in astronomy and mathematics were made during this time period, and it is no wonder. During this period, the Greeks began questioning the mathematical certainty of life, observing the universe around them and proposing new ideas. In fact, the Greeks questioned just about everything. They believed that pondering was the beginning of thinking. Before the Greeks, there was really no true science. The Egyptians practiced science, but it was only a practical science. For them, everything needed to serve a purpose. The Greeks, however, loved knowledge for its own sake. Many of the things that the Greeks discovered were of no practical use to them. Much of it was forgotten, not to be uncovered for hundreds of years. Once rediscovered, however, much of what they had learned became the beginnings of modern science and philosophy.

Many great thinkers lived during the Hellenistic period. These include the historian Polybius; the mathematician Euclid, who is almost single-handedly

Known as the Father of Geometry, Euclid was the author of Elements, *the undisputed authority on geometry for more than 2,000 years.*

responsible for modern geometry; the geographers Eratosthenes (he accurately calculated the circumference of Earth) and Poseidonius; and the linguist Dionysius Thrax. However, no list of great Hellenistic thinkers would be complete if it did not include the great Archimedes. In one of the greatest civilizations ever and among some of the most brilliant thinkers, he still stands out from all the rest. He was undoubtedly one of the most intelligent people in history. The following chapters will travel through the life, the education, and the discoveries of this great mathematician, Archimedes.

CHAPTER ONE

ARCHIMEDES'S EARLY YEARS

The specific details of Archimedes's life are hazy. Of course, he lived many thousands of years ago, and many records from that time have been lost. Unfortunately, we do not have a first-hand account: Archimedes never wrote about his own life. Only one biography is known to have been written during his time, and that has been lost to history. What is not lost, however, are his contributions to science and mathematics. Today, many historians rank Archimedes as one of the three greatest mathematicians ever to have lived. The others are physicist and mathematician Sir Isaac Newton and Carl Friedrich Gauss, known as the father of modern mathematics.

Isaac Newton was an English physicist and mathematician who played an important role in the scientific revolution of the seventeenth century.

NEWTON AND GAUSS

Much of Archimedes's work in the field of mathematics would be used as a foundation for later mathematicians. Two of the most notable are Sir Isaac Newton (1642–1727) and Carl Friedrich Gauss (1777–1855).

Sir Isaac Newton was a seventeenth-century British physicist and mathematician and was instrumental in that era's scientific revolution. As a mathematician, his work was a foundation for the development of calculus. Newton was also responsible for three of physics' fundamental laws of motion and the law of gravity. Until Albert Einstein formulated his theories of relativity, Newton's work was the commonly accepted scientific view of the world.

German scientist and mathematician Carl Friedrich Gauss is a major contributor to modern mathematics and science. A child prodigy, Gauss made a number of mathematical discoveries in his teenage years. He spent the rest of his life innovating and stretching the boundaries of mathematical knowledge, particularly in the realm of number theory. Gauss devoted later years to the study of astronomy.

A MATHEMATIC DESTINY

Unlike Newton and Gauss, Archimedes's background and upbringing probably steered him directly into the field of mathematics. It is safe to assume that Archimedes was aware of the importance of precise mathematics from an early age. For one, Archimedes's father, Pheidias, who was also born in Syracuse, had been a well-known astronomer and mathematician. This most surely gave Archimedes an interest in science. This may also explain why Archimedes found the sun, the moon, and the planets so fascinating.

Archimedes was born into the leisured upper class. Historians believe that Archimedes received a thorough grounding in mathematics as part of his education. The Greeks loved knowledge, and they sent their sons to school to become knowledgeable Greek citizens. In school, it is likely that Archimedes was exposed to knowledge originating in Egypt, Babylon, and Greece.

Historians believe that Archimedes had a typical education. During that time, students learned the twenty-seven letters of the Greek alphabet. These letters also doubled as numerals (a little mark next to the letter showed the reader that the letter was being used as a number). Students studied the epic poems of Homer, Solon's laws, and Aesop's fables. In addition to astronomy, students also studied music and drawing. They were taught military strategy and how to use weapons. Since the Greeks believed that a good mind needed a strong body, students learned how

Greek students during Archimedes's time would have studied Aesop's fables. Fables teach moral lessons.

to wrestle, box, run, jump, and throw a spear. Also, they learned how to swim and dive.

During the third century BCE, Syracuse was the hub of commerce, science, and art. In the days of Archimedes, as many as five hundred thousand people lived in Syracuse. In fact, it was the largest city in the ancient world. Archimedes probably walked through the crowded markets, packed with merchants selling books and other goods, up the narrow, busy streets, and down to the prosperous shipyards filled with workers. He may have stood on the docks, packed with Greek ships, watching as they were coming and going from places like Egypt and Athens. Growing up in such a rich area would have definitely helped to develop Archimedes's natural curiosity and his fondness for solving problems.

It was in the social and economic order of things that Archimedes should become a mathematician of some sort. Whether he would be an amateur or brilliant remained to be seen. Time would reveal that

Archimedes was to become the latter: a gifted genius in the field of mathematics. There are even those who would say that he became the greatest mathematician ever.

Archimedes was educated in the arts and sciences. He also learned military strategy.

HIERO'S IMPACT ON ARCHIMEDES

Archimedes is believed to have belonged to the nobility of Syracuse and was related in some way to Hiero II, the king of Syracuse. Archimedes certainly had an intimate relationship with Hiero and his son, Gelon, both of whom had the utmost respect for him.

King Hiero II ruled Syracuse from 270 BCE to 215 BCE, almost the entire span of Archimedes's adult life. Hiero was a peace-loving ruler in a time when rulers were often prone to war. In fact, many historians believe

The Temple of Apollo still stands in Sicily today. The ancient city of Syracuse was at its peak during King Hiero's reign.

that Hiero was able to finish out his rule without ever killing, injuring, or exiling a single citizen. Hiero built temples, a theater, and new fortifications all, according to reports, without having to issue heavy taxes on his citizens. The beginning of Hiero's rule marked a golden age

King Hiero II was an important ruler of Syracuse and the force behind many of Archimedes's inventions.

KING HIERO II

We have King Hiero II to thank for many of Archimedes's achievements. His long and peaceful reign allowed Archimedes to focus on mathematics. In addition, he asked his good friend to help him solve several problems that resulted in some of Archimedes's greatest inventions.

Hiero came to power by working his way up the military ladder, then overthrowing the city's leader. By marrying the daughter of an influential citizen, he reinforced his status. Hiero was named king of the city by defending Syracuse from mercenaries in 265 BCE.

The following year brought the First Punic War, during which Syracuse found itself under siege over the fight for control of Sicily. Hiero forged an alliance with Rome, a decision that ushered in a long period of calm for Syracuse. In fact, for the rest of Hiero's life and reign, Syracuse enjoyed peace and prosperity.

Hiero took advantage of this by improving Syracuse through various public works projects, many of which remain today. He also bolstered Syracuse from a military standpoint—with great assistance and input from Archimedes.

In 215 BCE, at the age of ninety, after a fifty-five-year rule, Hiero died. His grandson, Hieronymos, succeeded him, but without the respected and beloved king at its helm, Syracuse was never the same.

for Syracuse. The treaty that Hiero had negotiated with Rome during the First Punic War ensured a peaceful and prosperous reign for Hiero as well as for the people of Syracuse.

Hiero's long, peaceful reign had a major impact on the life of Archimedes. It allowed him to pursue his studies and further his knowledge. Whenever Hiero faced a difficult situation, he sought Archimedes's help. The king asked Archimedes questions about everything from military matters to sailing issues. It seems that Archimedes made a hobby out of solving the king's most difficult problems. Some of the questions posed by the king may have even led Archimedes to some of his greatest discoveries.

CHAPTER TWO

A THIRST FOR KNOWLEDGE

As a boy in Syracuse, Archimedes was a voracious learner. The academic opportunities there, however, were limited. Once he had exhausted the knowledge his hometown had to offer, he left Sicily for the city of Alexandria, Egypt. Located at the mouth of the mighty Nile River, Alexandria was Egypt's northernmost port city and a hub for civilization's great minds. It was a big journey, but one of utmost necessity to Archimedes.

In order to reach Alexandria, Archimedes had to sail across the Mediterranean Sea. This was not as simple as it would be today. During Archimedes's time, sea travel was still a dangerous endeavor. Ships were small, wooden vessels called round ships, which had a stationary, square sail that could not be turned to the direction of the wind. This meant that the ship's course was determined by the direction in which the wind blew, potentially adding considerable time to every journey. And ship crews had no compasses or sea charts to guide them. Adding to the challenge of sea travel was the threat of pirates.

Travel by sea was particularly dangerous during the time Archimedes lived. It is remarkable that he journeyed to Alexandria to further his studies.

It is even more extraordinary that Archimedes made the decision to leave his home and undertake such a journey when he was still quite young. Traveling to Alexandria must have meant a lot to Archimedes. He risked so much to get there. However, knowing his great thirst for knowledge it is not surprising that Archimedes was willing to take that risk.

THE HELLENISTIC CENTER

Alexandria offered Archimedes the best education to be found anywhere in the Greek world. The city was still young when Archimedes arrived. However, Alexandria had already become the center for Greek culture and learning. When Alexander the Great died, his generals divided the empire, including all of the lands he had conquered, extending from Greece and Egypt all the way into India. Ptolemy I took Egypt and turned Alexandria into a city of artistic and academic importance.

Ptolemy built the great library of Alexandria. His aim was to gather into it all the known books in the world. Though that may have been an unrealistic goal, the library did contain an impressive half million books or more. Attached to the library was a museum, which Ptolemy built in about 300 BCE. The term "museum," which is still used today, literally means "place of muses." It was a place where scholars could ponder, or think about, intellectual ideas. Many did just that, producing encyclopedias of knowledge. Archimedes was able to study many texts at the great library and museum.

Alexandria's world-renowned library, where so many ancient scholars studied, was commissioned by Ptolemy. The facility made Alexandria a great intellectual and cultural center.

Today, scholars would consider the museum in Alexandria a great university. The school excelled all others of its time in science, philosophy, poetry, and music. The museum was also rich in scientific facilities. It had observatories, consulting rooms, botanical and zoological gardens, and anatomy lecture halls, to name a few. To this cultural center came scientists from all around the civilized world.

EUCLID AND GEOMETRY

While in Alexandria, Archimedes studied the works of the great geometer Euclid. Euclid, who lived in Alexandria from 330 to 275 BCE, was Greek like Archimedes. Euclid died before Archimedes was old enough to go to Alexandria, but his followers carried on his work at the museum.

THE BOX OF ARCHIMEDES

Archimedes loved geometry so much that even his games involved geometrical shapes. Archimedes wrote about a game he developed called the Box of Archimedes. The game was a sort of blank puzzle made up of fourteen ivory pieces. The polygon-shaped puzzle pieces fit together to form a rectangle. One of the objects of the game was to re-form the rectangle after mixing up the pieces. Another popular activity was to rearrange the pieces to form other geometrical shapes or interesting things, such as ele-phants, trees, or boats. The Greeks called the game *stomachion*, which appropriately means "something that drives you wild."

The stomachion is a dissection puzzle described in the Archimedes Palimpsest.

Euclid was both a great mathematician and teacher. He is best known for having gathered all of the mathematical theories that were known before him and tying them together with his own important work in geometry. He combined all of these ideas in an ordered and logical way in his book *The Elements*. There are thirteen books of Euclid's elements. Within these books are plane geometry (geometry that deals with one- and two-dimensional shapes such as circles, lines, and polygons); the nature and properties of whole numbers (numbers such as 0, 1, 2, 3, and so on); solid geometry (three-dimensional solids such as spheres or cubes); and the theory of proportions and magnitude. Geometry students used *The Elements* for more than two thousand years, and it undoubtedly had an influence on the work of Archimedes.

APPLIED AND THEORETICAL MATHEMATICS

Prior to the Hellenistic period, there were no places like Alexandria, which offered different schools of thought. For example, there was a difference between Egyptian science and Greek science.

Greek mathematics was more theoretical: the Greeks sought to find the principles, or truths, of mathematics.

Egyptian mathematics, however, was focused on applied mathematics: more practical and useful for everyday life. The Egyptian mathematicians were

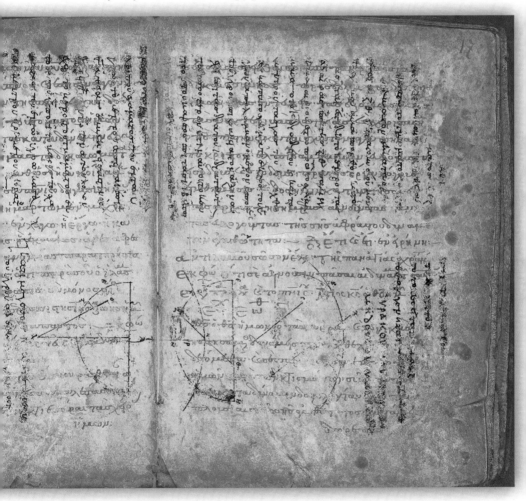

A tenth-century copy of Archimedes's work was written over by monks in the thirteenth century. By carefully erasing the monks' religious text, Archimedes's work is now visible.

concerned with things like land measurement, construction, and irrigation. By the third century BCE, the school in Alexandria was noted for such practical devices as water clocks, hydraulic devices, and machines driven by compressed air.

While studying in Alexandria, Archimedes developed a taste for applied mathematics and practical devices. In fact, Alexandria is where he invented his first practical device.

It is believed, however, that Archimedes valued his theoretical work much more than his practical works. First-century Greek biographer Plutarch, who wrote accounts of many famous Greeks and Romans, writes that Archimedes thought of applied mathematics as ignoble, or shameful, and that it was not worthy of pursuit. Some historians believe that this may not have been true at all. They believe that Plutarch may have been attributing his own feelings to Archimedes.

INFLUENTIAL COLLEAGUES

In Alexandria, Archimedes studied physics, astronomy, and mathematics with many other great minds of the time. Archimedes became life-long friends with two men: Conon, of the Greek island of Samos, and Eratosthenes of Cyrene (now Shahhat, Libya). Conon taught mathematics to Archimedes at the museum. Not only was Conon a gifted mathematician, but he was also one of the great early astronomers. He studied the sun's eclipses and is credited with the discovery of the constellation Coma

Berenices. Archimedes respected Conon very much, both as a mathematician and as a friend. In fact, Conon was one of the greatest influences in Archimedes's life.

Archimedes's friend Eratosthenes settled in Alexandria and became the head of the famous library. Eratosthenes was the first to estimate Earth's circumference and tilt. He also calculated the sizes of the sun and moon and their distance from Earth. Eratosthenes also became a noted geographer. As such, he was the first to indicate longitude and latitude on a map. Conon and Eratosthenes seem to be the only two men of that time that Archimedes felt would understand his work. For the rest of his life, Archimedes corresponded with these men, exchanging ideas. In fact, some of Archimedes's finest work is found in letters to Conon. After Conon's death, Archimedes corresponded with one of Conon's pupils, Dositheus. With these three men, Archimedes discussed many problems and their solutions.

After studying in Alexandria, Archimedes returned home to his beloved Syracuse, where he spent the rest of his life. However, his studies in Alexandria became the foundation on which he built his career as a scientist and mathematician. He went on to discover many monumental things in both theoretical and applied mathematics. Archimedes wrote about his findings in various papers, called treatises. Of the treatises he wrote, only ten have survived. In his most recently discovered treatise, *The Method*, Archimedes describes

ERATOSTHENES

Most of what we know about the great geographer and astronomer Eratosthenes comes from the writings of Pappus of Alexandria. Known as Eratosthenes of Cyrene, he was born around 276 BCE in Cyrene (now Libya). He moved to Alexandria around 255 and, as head of the city's library, had much influence on its academics and culture.

Eratosthenes created a prime number tool, known as the sieve of Eratosthenes, that is used in number theory research even today. The method is as follows: After arranging the natural numbers in numerical order, strike out the number 1. Following the number 2, strike out every second number. Following the number 3, strike out every third number, and continue in this pattern of striking out every nth number following the number n. His other contributions include a calendar; writings on subjects as varied as science, drama, and ethics; and geographical maps. He was also a poet. Perhaps most important, Eratosthenes devised a method for calculating Earth's circumference. Experts today believe his work was not entirely accurate, but his contributions to astronomy are not in doubt.

Plagued by blindness in his later years, Eratosthenes is believed to have died by self-imposed starvation around 194 BCE.

Eratosthenes made the first-known measurement of Earth's size. He became the director of Alexandria's great library.

the process of his discovery of mathematic truths. In this treatise, discovered in 1906, Archimedes explains how he first designed a way to attack a problem, then masterfully organized a plan, then sternly eliminated everything that was not immediately relevant to his purpose, and then, finally, finished the work. Archimedes wrote many treatises about his findings. Some of these are on display in museums today. Archimedes's surviving treatises are mathematical works of art, and it is unfortunate that many more have been lost.

CHAPTER THREE

ARCHIMEDES, PURE MATHEMATICS, AND INFINITY

Thanks to his studies in Alexandria, Archimedes's knowledge of the study of mathematics was quite broad and, indeed, he became a very modern thinker. He understood both theoretical and applied mathematics. Archimedes was very fond of theoretical, also known as pure, mathematics. He worked with arithmetic, which is the study of numbers; trigonometry, which calculates the relationship between distances and directions; and geometry, which analyzes the nature of and properties of shapes.

FREEDOM TO EXPLORE

Of all the ancients, Archimedes had the greatest freedom of his contemporaries in his

The ancient Greek philosopher Plato formulated many ideas that were instrumental in the development of Western culture.

exploration of mathematics. This was due to the stature, strength, and time that came with being born into a higher social class. Many other ancient mathematicians were restricted to philosophical rules set forth by Plato. Plato, a philosopher who died sixty years before Archimedes's birth, believed that the study of geometry required only a straightedge and a pair of compasses. Today, freedom to explore different ideas is a privilege that some mathematicians may take for granted. However, this freedom was hard-won by centuries of previous mathematicians.

Archimedes spent most of his time contemplating new problems to solve. He drew geometrical figures in the dirt and even in the ashes of extinguished fires. His freedom to explore mathematics resulted in some very bold discoveries that were far beyond his time. He invented his own counting system and developed new

ARCHIMEDES'S WORK SURFACES

When speaking about Archimedes, most will mention his tendency to write on whatever surfaces he could find. Anything and everything served as a blackboard for Archimedes. He scrawled ideas out on sawdust-covered floors and drew geometric shapes in the ashes

(continued on the next page)

(continued from previous page)

of extinguished fires. However, Archimedes did have other options. As a child in school, he would have been given a wax-covered wooden tablet on which to write. On it he would have scratched his letters with a sharp, pointed iron graver. When he was able to write very well, Archimedes would have been given a papyrus to write on. His pen would have been made from a reed, and the ink he dipped it in would have been made of gum and soot. Books were also surprisingly popular and common among the Greeks, even though the printing press would not be invented for another 1,800 years.

Why then did Archimedes spend hours sitting on the ground, drawing his diagrams in the dirt? The answer is, most geometers in his day worked like that. They had no pencils or erasers. Each sheet of papyrus was made by hand and was too valuable just to be scribbled on and then thrown away. Also it was difficult to change a diagram that had been cut into clay or scratched into a wax surface. It turns out that a surface of dirt, sand, or ash was ideal for drawing in this time when paper was scarce. With a simple sweep of his hand, Archimedes was able to smooth away any mistakes and start fresh with a new diagram.

ways to calculate the areas and volumes of geometric figures. Some of his mathematical methods closely resembled integral calculus, a very complicated branch of mathematics discovered two thousand years later. In fact, Archimedes's work with theoretical mathematics cleared up almost every geometric measuring problem that was left to be solved during his time.

CIRCLES, POLYGONS, AND PI

Archimedes conducted many studies of the circle. It was very important to him to find an accurate way to solve the area of this geometric shape. One way to do this is to make use of the ratio between the circumference (the distance around the circle) and the diameter (the distance from one side of the circle to the other.) This ratio, known as pi, is represented by the symbol π.

Pi got its name because it was the first letter of the Greek word *perimetros*, which means perimeter or circumference. The area of a circle can be calculated easily once the diameter is measured. The problem was that the ancients did not have an accurate number for pi. Archimedes sought to fix that.

Prior to Archimedes's work, the best value for pi came from the Egyptians. They figured it to be 3.16. However, that number, and all other values of pi known before it, had been estimates based on measurements. Archimedes would be the first to calculate the value mathematically.

Archimedes described his work with circles in his treatise *Measurement of the Circle*. In it, he describes how he used two polygons (figures with three or more sides) to find an approximation for pi. Archimedes drew one of the polygons just inside the circle and one just outside the

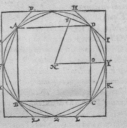

Archimedes described his methods for calculating pi in his treatise Measurement of the Circle.

circle. The area of the circle would lie somewhere between the areas of the two polygons.

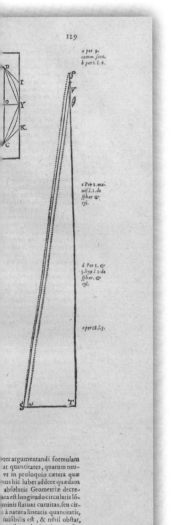

Archimedes then measured the length of the polygons' perimeters. By increasing the number of sides that the polygons had, Archimedes was able to bring the perimeters of the polygons closer to the circumference of the circle. Archimedes began with six-sided polygons, which touched the circle at six points each. He then increased this number to twelve, then twenty-four, and so on. In order to have enough points on the polygons so that every one of their points corresponded to a point on the circle, Archimedes would have had to continue increasing the number of sides forever. This is because there are an infinite number of points on a circle. That means that there is no end to the number of points. Archimedes would have had to increase the number of sides of his polygons forever!

Many ancient mathematicians did not believe that infinity was truly infinite. They believed that with enough hard work and patience, infinity could be reached. Archimedes did not share this belief, however. He knew that infinity was uncountable, beyond reach.

THE CATTLE PROBLEM

Around the time that Archimedes was studying in Alexandria, another young man, Apollonius, was also there. Apollonius worked with conics—the curves you get when you slice a cone. Today, Apollonius is known for naming these curves: ellipse, parabola, and hyperbola.

Though Archimedes and Apollonius may not have met, they were certainly familiar with each other's work. It seems that Apollonius rubbed Archimedes the wrong way. Apparently, Apollonius tried to outdo some of Archimedes's achievements. Historians believe that Apollonius annoyed Archimedes so much that Archimedes challenged the young scientist with an extremely difficult problem.

Archimedes's problem is known today as "the cattle problem." In the problem, Helios, the sun god, had a herd of bulls and cows. Some of them were yellow, some white, some black, and some spotted. Archimedes established seven relationships between the number of each color and the sex. For example, he said that the number of white cows was 7/12 of the number of all the black cows and bulls together.

In addition to the seven relationships, such as this, there were also two special requirements. The first requirement was that the yel-

The great geometer Appolonius of Perga wrote the groundbreaking treatise Conics.

low and spotted bulls grouped together had to form a triangular shape. Second, the black and white bulls, when grouped together, had to form a square. The challenge of the problem was to figure out how many oxen there were.

Most historians doubt whether either Archimedes or Apollonius actually ever solved the problem. In fact, it took more than two thousand years and the world's fastest computers to solve it. Though the question itself is simple, the solution is actually quite complicated. It turns out that the smallest possible answer for the herd's total size is a 202,545-digit number. Now that's a lot of cattle!

Therefore, he stopped adding sides to his polygons when they had ninety-six sides each. He then found the perimeter of the inside polygon, as well as that for the one on the outside—no easy task in Archimedes's day. In this way, Archimedes calculated pi to be between the values of 3 10/71 and 3 1/7. As decimals, these numbers are about 3.141 and 3.143, respectively. Archimedes's value for pi was correct to two decimal places. Later mathematicians gradually improved on Archimedes's figure by using polygons with more and more sides so that they fit more closely the shape of a circle. Today, the value of pi is calculated to be 3.14159~, or rounded off to 3.142.

ARCHIMEDES'S NUMBER SYSTEM

One of Archimedes's great contributions to mathematics was that he eliminated the fear of using large numbers. Not only did many ancient Greeks not believe in infinity, they counted up to 10,000 only, what they called a myriad. They also believed that no number existed that was high enough to count the number of grains of sand it would take to fill the universe. In those days, people thought that the universe was the space between the sun, the moon, and the five planets known at that time: Venus, Mercury, Mars, Jupiter, and Saturn. Since no one could actually sit down and count the sand, they assumed that the number must have been so high that it did not exist. In his short book *The Sand Reckoner*, addressed to King Gelon of Syracuse, Archimedes wrote:

Determined to prove the existence of large numbers, Archimedes set out to count the number of grains of sand in the universe.

Many people believe, King Gelon, that the grains of sand are infinite in multitude; and I mean by the sand not only that which exists around Syracuse and the rest of Sicily, but also that which is found in every region, whether inhabited or uninhabited. Others think that although their number is not without limit, no number can ever be named which will be greater than the number of grains of sand. But I shall try to prove to you that among the numbers which I have named there are those which exceed the number of grains in a heap of sand the size not only of the earth, but even of the universe.

Archimedes loved a challenge, so he decided to try to count the sand needed to fill the universe. To show that he was not being easy on himself, he chose a very fine sand to fill the universe. First, Archimedes counted the number of grains of sand that would form a cluster the size of a poppy seed. He figured that one poppy would not contain more than ten thousand grains of sand. Next, he counted the number of poppy seeds that would equal the size of a man's finger. Then, he calculated how many fingers it would take to fill a stadium. Archimedes continued in this way until he had his answer. In *The Sand Reckoner*, Archimedes estimated the number of grains of sand needed to fill the universe to be less than 1×10^{63} (that is "one" followed by sixty-three zeros). Today, calculations using a sphere with the radius of Pluto's orbit put the number of grains of sand needed to fill our universe at about 1×10^{51}.

In order to convey his very large number, Archimedes had to develop his own numbering system, as numbers did not exist to count that high during the third century BCE. Using his system, Archimedes was capable of expressing, in language, numbers up to one followed by 80,000 million million zeros. Archimedes noted in *The Sand Reckoner* that even though this number is larger than any number the Greeks had seen before, it still did not come close to infinity.

Though Archimedes's number system never caught on, it did serve to show that tremendously large numbers can be formed by multiplying smaller numbers together over and over. Today, we use a number system called exponential notation to describe large numbers. This system multiplies tens together to get larger numbers. For instance 10^2 means 10×10, or 100. Here, ten is called the base number and two is called the exponent. Likewise 10^5, or 10 to the 5th power, is $10 \times 10 \times 10 \times 10 \times 10$, or 100,000. We most likely owe this modern, much simpler, system of expressing numbers to Archimedes.

ARCHIMEDES'S METHOD OF EXHAUSTION

Of all the branches of mathematics he studied, Archimedes especially loved geometry. Some of the geometrical problems that Archimedes solved concerned the areas and volumes of geometric figures, both plane and solid. Plane figures are two-

dimensional and flat, having the dimensions of length and width. Planes can be drawn on paper. In addition to the circle, Archimedes also studied plane figures like triangles, spirals, parabolas, and ellipses. He wrote about these in his treatises *Measurement of a Circle*, *Quadrature of the Parabola*, and *On Spirals*.

Solid figures are three-dimensional (having the dimensions of length, width, and height) and take up space. Some examples of the solid figures that Archimedes studied are spheres, cylinders, and cones. He recorded his work with solids in his writings *On the Sphere and Cylinder* and *On Conoids and Spheroids*.

Archimedes devised new ways to determine the formulas for the areas and

Archimedes's work on circles is described in detail in his treatise Measurement of a Circle, *a fragment of a longer work.*

volumes of these and other plane and solid figures. He used a strategy, called the method of exhaustion. This method was an early form of integration, a type of calculus. To determine the areas of sections bound by geometric figures, such as parabolas and ellipses, Archimedes broke the sections into smaller and smaller rectangular areas and then added the areas together. Archimedes used the method of exhaustion to find his value for pi. He elaborated upon the method of exhaustion in his treatise *The Method*. Amazingly, this anticipated the development of integral calculus by two thousand years!

CHAPTER FOUR

NECESSITY IS THE MOTHER OF INVENTION

A lthough Archimedes preferred to be known for his achievements in pure mathematics, he was called upon often to use his mathematical prowess for practical applications. It was King Hiero, with whom he had a close relationship, who often commissioned Archimedes to invent creations that would solve Hiero's problems. Requests from the king resulted in inventions such as pulleys and levers that could move tremendous weights and astonishing arrays of war machines, such as cranes, and catapultlike missile launchers.

Archimedes also used applied mathematics in his work on theoretical mathematics. Out of necessity, he would create inventions in order to prove his theories. He cared less about these practical inventions than he did the theories behind them. Still, he has left a mark on the field of applied mathematics. Many historians, including Plutarch, believe Archimedes was one of the greatest mechanical geniuses of all time.

USING A SCREW TO SOLVE IRRIGATION PROBLEMS

While he was studying in Alexandria, Egypt, Archimedes discovered a very useful and practical tool, a device now known as the Archimedean screw. This invention was used as a means of pumping water out of the Nile River. The Nile, which flows through Egypt, is the longest river in the world. Every year, the Nile overflowed, giving the land around it plenty of water for the farmers to grow their crops. However, during times when there was no rain, crops suffered. In order to irrigate their fields, the Egyptian farmers had to carry water in buckets from the river. Watering their fields in this way took a lot of time and effort. Archimedes's screw, however, made their lives a whole lot easier.

The Archimedean screw is a hollow tube, or cylinder, that is open at each end. Inside the cylinder is a continuous screw that forms spiral chambers. It works when one end of the screw is placed in the water and the other end is turned. The turning motion pushes the water into the spiral chambers, forcing it to flow upward, from one chamber to the next until it finally spills out the top and onto the land.

The Archimedean screw, designed by Archimedes to pump water from the Nile, is still used today.

Some Egyptian farmers still use Archimedes's screw to irrigate their fields. It ranges in size from a quarter of an inch (6.35 millimeters) to 12 feet in diameter (3.65 meters). In the Netherlands, as well as other countries where unwanted water needs to be drained from the surface of the land, the screw is used in reverse. It forces the water from the land, into the spiral chambers, and finally back into the canals.

In Archimedes's day, his invention was used mostly for irrigation. But there were other uses as well—seamen used the screw to bail water out of their ships. Though Archimedes's screw may not be widely used today, many modern inventions are based on the design and principle behind it. Motorboat and airplane propellers are quite similar to Archimedes's screw. Motorboat propellers push water through the propeller behind them, driving the boat forward. Airplane propellers, called airscrews, move planes forward by pushing air backward. The Archimedean screw was the first machine that Archimedes invented, but it was not the last.

FORCE AND THE COMPOUND PULLEY

Archimedes believed in theoretical mechanics, the in-depth description and explanation of the motion of objects in the universe. It was with theoretical mechanics that Archimedes solved the problem of moving a large weight with a small amount of force. This is done by means of what is called a compound pulley.

A pulley is a machine consisting of a rope wrapped around a wheel. This machine can turn or reverse the

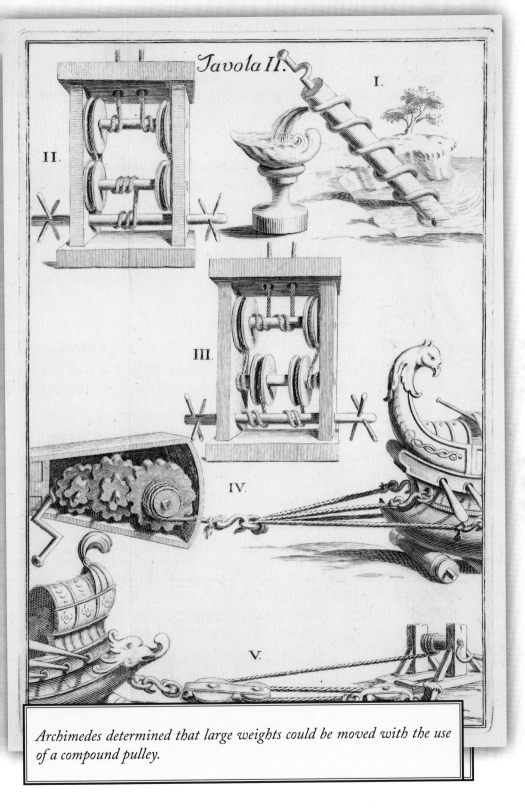

Archimedes determined that large weights could be moved with the use of a compound pulley.

direction of a force. Compound pulleys use two or more pulleys to divide the amount of force needed to perform a task.

Compound pulleys are such useful machines that they are still used today. If you walk into an auto mechanic's garage you might see a large compound pulley used to lift the engines out of cars. Compound pulleys are also used at construction sites to lift large quantities of heavy building material. These machines haven't changed much since Archimedes's day.

Archimedes declared to King Hiero that any amount of weight could be moved by any amount of force, no matter the disparity between the two. Even a great weight could be moved with just a small force. He even boasted to the king, as quoted in Pappus of Alexandria's *Collectio*, "Give me a lever long enough, and a fulcrum strong enough, and I will single-handedly move the world."

Though Archimedes greatly valued pure, mathematical reasoning, it seems that King Hiero felt that mathematical theories were nothing until applied to practical things. To prove his statement to Hiero, Archimedes filled one of the king's large ships with many passengers and cargo. He then sat far away and effortlessly moved the ship through the water by simply pulling on the end of a compound pulley.

Archimedes based the design for his ship-moving device on the lever and fulcrum. Levers are machines that reduce the amount of force needed to do work by spreading the force over a greater distance. Called simple machines, levers have only two parts: the handle and the fulcrum. The handle is the part that is pushed or pulled, and the fulcrum is the point on which the lever turns or balances. A pulley is a type of lever. A fork is another example of a lever, the fulcrum being the point at which your fingers hold it. Scissors are an example of two levers put together. Archimedes described his work with levers in his treatise *On the Equilibrium of Planes.*

The account of Archimedes moving the ship with his pulley system first appeared in written form nearly three hundred years after the incident occurred. For this reason, many historians believe that the story could have changed over time or been exaggerated with the telling and retelling. However, most scientists believe that in order for Archimedes to move a large ship filled with cargo and passengers, he must have used a fairly complex pulley system. Archimedes may have even used some of his other inventions in the process, such as the windlass (a simple crank-and-axle arrangement commonly used to raise a bucket from a well) or the worm gear (a device in which a screwlike "worm" meshes with the teeth of a gear). These inventions attached to a compound pulley, scientists agree, could have gotten the job done.

HYDROSTATICS AND SPECIFIC GRAVITY

After coming to power, Hiero wished to present his favorite temple with a gift, a golden *stephane.* Similar to a crown but wide at the forehead and narrow at the sides, stephanes were often seen on the statues of Greek goddesses. Hiero ordered a goldsmith to make one out of

At the behest of Hiero, Archimedes used hydrostatics to determine the purity of the gold on the king's crown.

pure gold. However, when the crown was finished, Hiero suspected that the goldsmith had cheated him by mixing the gold with a less valuable metal.

As he so often did when faced with a difficult problem, Hiero turned to Archimedes for a solution. Historians are not exactly sure how Archimedes went about testing the king's crown. He would have had to devise a way of testing it without damaging it, but still there are probably several ways he could have completed the task. As with most of his practical ideas, Archimedes failed to write down what he did.

The story of how Archimedes solved this problem was first recorded two or three centuries after Archimedes's time. It was first mentioned in a book about architecture that was published in about 30 BCE by the Roman architect Vitruvius. As the story goes, Archimedes's inspiration came one day while he was taking a bath. As he was getting into the tub, he noticed that water spilled over the sides of the tub as he submerged himself. Upon further experimentation, he realized that anything placed in the tub would displace a volume of water that was equal to its own volume. Volume is the amount of space that an object occupies. Archimedes also realized that when samples of two different materials weighed the same, the denser material displaced less water than the less dense material. Density is the mass contained within a unit volume.

If two objects weigh the same, the denser material would take up less volume than the less dense material. All Archimedes needed to do to solve the king's problem was

After discovering that King Hiero's crown was not as dense as pure gold, Archimedes explained that the king had been cheated.

to compare the amount of water displaced by the crown to the amount of water displaced by pure gold of equal weight. According to the story, Archimedes was so excited by his discovery that he jumped from the bath, forgetting to clothe himself, and ran naked through the streets of Syracuse shouting, "Eureka!," meaning, "I have found it!"

Vitruvius states that Archimedes obtained a block of gold and a block of silver that weighed the same as the crown. He then compared the volumes of the three objects (the gold, the silver, and the crown). Archimedes did this by filling a jug to the brim with water, dropping each object, in turn, into the jug, and carefully measuring how much water each object displaced. Gold has greater density than silver. Therefore, a sample of gold would displace less water than a sample of silver that weighs the same amount. In the same way, the sample of pure gold would displace a smaller volume of water than an impure crown. If the crown were made of pure gold, it should displace the same amount of water as the block of pure gold.

Upon doing his experiment, Archimedes saw that the block of pure gold displaced less water than the crown. This meant that the crown was less dense than the gold and was not pure. Indeed, the king had been cheated.

Though the fate of the goldsmith is unknown, what is far more important is what Archimedes had done. He had discovered the science of hydrostatics. The word "hydrostatics" comes from the Greek words *hydro*, meaning "water," and *statikos*, meaning "causing to stand." The science of hydrostatics deals with the laws that govern how liquids behave when they are at rest, or not moving. Archimedes was so far ahead of his time with the concept of hydrostatics that it was not until the 1800s that any new discoveries were made in this field.

From his bathtub experience, Archimedes came to understand the law of buoyancy. He described his findings in a treatise entitled *On Floating Bodies.* Buoyancy is the name for the upward lifting force of water. Today, this law is known as Archimedes's principle. Archimedes's principle states that when an object is placed in a fluid, it is buoyed up by a force that is equal to the weight of the fluid it displaces. Archimedes's body probably took the place of about 2 cubic feet (0.05 cubic meters) of water when he submerged himself in his bath. Therefore, his body was buoyed up by a force equal to the weight of 2 cubic feet (0.05 cu m) of water.

Archimedes is also credited for the idea of specific gravity. Before Archimedes, scientists were not quite sure how to compare accurately the densities of different objects. Specific gravity accomplished this. Specific gravity is the weight of an object relative to water. For example, gold is nineteen times as heavy as an equal volume of water, so its specific gravity is nineteen. Silver has a specific gravity of eleven. Archimedes found the idea of specific gravity very useful when he was talking about buoyancy. He showed that anything with a specific gravity less than one would float in water, while anything with a specific gravity greater than one would sink. Based on those findings, it is safe to say that no matter whether Hiero's crown was made of silver or gold, it definitely would have sunk.

THE LEVER AND GRAVITY

Gravity is the force that pulls objects back toward the Earth. Gravity also pulls two objects together. Most scientists agree that the first real understanding of gravity came during the seventeenth century with Sir Isaac Newton. However, two thousand years before Newton, Greek scientists already had a faint idea about gravity and its effects here on Earth. Archimedes experimented with equilibrium, or balance, and centers of gravity for both solid and plane figures. His studies on centers of gravity,

MOBILES

Archimedes's discovery about levers was later applied to such things as weight-lifting equipment and seesaws. You can study what Archimedes learned about levers by making a mobile. Making a mobile is an easy way to learn about centers of gravity. When you make a mobile, you use sticks, some thread, a ruler, and some small objects you can weigh. Each mobile is a lever in equilibrium. When you make a mobile, you have to spend time finding the right positions to hang the objects so that the mobile is evenly balanced. You can make your mobile as simple or as fancy as you wish. You just have to follow the principles Archimedes discovered.

explained in his treatise *On the Equilibrium of Planes,* formed the foundation for the science of theoretical mechanics.

Archimedes began his investigation of the center of gravity with the lever. The basic law of the lever may have been known before Archimedes's time, but he was the first to prove it. Imagine a seesaw, which is the simplest type of lever. Archimedes showed that equal weights at equal but opposite distances from the fulcrum of such a lever will balance. Equal weights at unequal distances, however, will not balance. In that case, the weight that is farther from the fulcrum will tilt its side of the lever down. Archimedes also showed that if the two weights balance and additional weight is added to one of the weights, the side on which the additional weight was added will go down. Likewise, if the two weights are even and weight is taken away from one side, the side holding the weight that was not changed will go down.

From balancing weights against one another like

Archimedes did not invent the lever, but he was the first to prove the basic law of the lever through his experiments determining the center of gravity.

this, Archimedes moved on to balancing parts of objects. By doing this, he was able to find the balancing point, or center of gravity, for many different shapes. All objects

Archimedes's discoveries about the center of gravity through his work with levers are just some of his great contributions to applied mathematics.

will balance on their center of gravity. For some shapes, the center of gravity is obvious. For a circle, the center of gravity is the center. However, Archimedes proved that an object's center of gravity is not always its center. If an object has a heavy end and a light end, the center of gravity will lie closer to the heavy end.

A spoon is a good example of this. If you were to balance a spoon on your finger, you would have to place your finger closer to the head of the spoon (the heavy end). The point on the spoon on which it would balance on your finger is its center of gravity.

Archimedes showed that the center of gravity for a square or a rectangle is the point at which lines drawn between the corners cross. A triangle's center of gravity is found by drawing lines from each corner to the center of the opposite side. The center of gravity is the point at which the lines cross. Archimedes also found the centers of gravity for more complicated shapes. One example of a complicated shape for which he found the center of gravity is a segment of a parabola. A parabola is a curve, and a segment of a parabola is the shape that would be made if the parabola were cut off by a straight line.

IN DEFENSE OF SYRACUSE

The people of Syracuse wondered how long it would be before Rome and Carthage would battle for control of Syracuse. In order to protect his city, King Hiero signed a treaty with the Romans, pledging friendship and cooperation. In return, the Romans offered protection from

ARCHIMEDES'S HEAT RAYS

One of the many legends concerning Archimedes holds that he was able to use heat rays as a weapon simply by using mirrors in a creative way. Supposedly, by positioning mirrors to reflect and redirect the sun's rays onto an object, that object would catch fire. Today, scientists do not believe that Archimedes was able to achieve such a feat, although that doesn't stop them from trying it themselves. Scientific experiments must hold up to replication to be considered sound. This means that another scientist should achieve the same results if conducting the experiment under identical conditions.

The popular television show *Myth-Busters* attempted to recreate Archimedes's heat ray combustion twice—in 2006 and again in 2010. Using conditions as close as possible to those of ancient Syracuse, both experiments resulted in what they call a "bust," or failure to replicate the phenomenon. Students at Massachusetts Institute of Technology (MIT) also tried to replicate the Archimedes experiment. They were able to get a sail to ignite, but only a bit and for a short time under conditions that most likely were not possible at sea.

The most successful replication of Archimedes's heat rays took place in the 1970s on a naval base near Athens. Mirrors were focused

Legend says that Archimedes used heat rays to ignite and destroy enemy ships, but this has not been replicated.

(continued from the previous page)

on a mockup of a ship constructed of plywood and coated with tar paint. The ship stand-in combusted within seconds. Scientists propose that ancient ships would have been coated with tar and that was most likely responsible for combustion.

While we can't be sure whether the story of Archimedes's heat rays is scientific truth or the stuff of legend, it seems the results have been greatly exaggerated, based on modern efforts to replicate the experiment. All agree, however, that the effect of such mirror reflections could have been useful in distracting or temporarily blinding the sailors on enemy ships.

the Carthaginians. Hiero wondered, however, how much help the Romans would actually provide in the event of an attack. Not wanting to find out, he turned, as he so often did when presented with a problem, to his trusted friend. Archimedes agreed to use his expertise to help Hiero devise a defense system for Syracuse. Though Archimedes disliked inventing practical machines, especially those meant for destruction, he saw the need to protect the city he loved and called home for so many years.

Among the machines he designed for the protection of the city were catapults that could hurl heavy stones over the city's walls. These catapults were constructed so ingeniously that they were equally effective at both long and short ranges. Archimedes also designed weapons that discharged showers of missiles through holes in the city walls.

Some of Archimedes's other inventions consisted of long, movable poles that projected beyond the city walls. These could either drop heavy weights on the enemy's ships or grab them with an iron hand or beaklike crane. The iron claws, which were controlled by ropes and other mechanisms, could destabilize or capsize an enemy ship. Once the sailors had fallen overboard, the claw could then release the ship, dropping it onto the jagged rocks below. It was also said that Archimedes developed a way to use mirrors to magnify the sun's heat onto enemy ships, causing them to catch fire. Modern-day experiments have shown that this would prove to be very difficult to accomplish, however. Many historians regard Archimedes's use of mirrors as nothing more than a legend.

Hiero was quite pleased with all of Archimedes's weapons. The king ordered that they be kept at the ready in the event of an emergency. When Hiero died around 215 BCE, the machines were in perfect working order, but they had yet to be used.

CHAPTER FIVE

WAR, MURDER, AND A LASTING LEGACY

The machines would prove useful, however, and within Archimedes's lifetime. Normally peaceful Syracuse would find itself under siege from Rome during the Second Punic War (218–201 BCE). This war had been years in the making. It was the resolution of unfinished business from the First Punic War (264–241 BCE), when Carthage was forced to surrender Sicily, among other isles, to Rome. This war had ended with a peace treaty, but Carthage feared that Rome would soon take over the Mediterranean entirely.

To prevent that from happening, Carthage occupied several towns in Spain and conquered a Roman town there. This did not sit well with Rome, which swiftly declared war on Carthage once again. The Second

Punic War was one of the ancient world's greatest military conflicts, and Archimedes would play an instrumental role in it.

SYRACUSE IS THREATENED

In 218 BCE, the Romans and the Carthaginians renewed their fighting, marking the start of the Second Punic War. At that time, Hannibal Barca, a military genius who had a lifelong disdain for Rome, led the Carthaginian troops. Under Hannibal's leadership, Carthage won the first round of battles against Rome. Although Hannibal's success was short-lived, it was enough to convince many Syracusans that they had formed an alliance with the wrong side.

By 215 BCE, the Second Punic War was in full swing. Rome and Carthage were fighting; Syracuse lay near the path of the Roman fleet. Hiero had honored his treaty with Rome while he lived. However, upon his death in 215 BCE, his fifteen-year-old grandson Hieronymus became ruler of Sicily. Hieronymus broke Syracuse's treaty with Rome and formed an alliance with Carthage. Alarmed by Syracuse's betrayal, Rome quickly turned its attention toward the great city. The Roman leader, Marcellus, anticipated a speedy victory over the Syracusans. However, this was not the case. The Syracusans were ready for the fight, thanks to Archimedes, who had used his knowledge of mathematics to build great weapons at King Hiero's request.

It was time for Archimedes to prepare the war machines for action. As the machines had been kept in

Carthaginian leader Hannibal Barca famously crossed the Alps with his troops, equipment, and elephants to defeat the Romans.

working order, none needed repair—they were ready to go. When the Romans arrived, the Syracusans awaited them, with Archimedes's inventions. The Romans attacked with a full frontal assault from both land and sea. However, they were no match for Archimedes's inventions. Archimedes's super-catapults hurled stones, each weighing more than a quarter of a ton. They demolished Marcellus's small catapults and mowed down his land forces. The cranelike beaks and iron claws reached down over the walls of the city, seized Marcellus's approaching ships, and sank or shattered them. The Romans tried for two years to capture Syracuse, but with no luck. Without victory in sight, Marcellus backed down. The Roman troops so feared Archimedes's inventions that if the Syracusans so much as dangled a rope over the city wall, the Romans recoiled in terror for fear that Archimedes was setting one of his inventions down upon them.

Syracuse was under siege for two years. Thanks to Archimedes's many inventions, the city did not fall. Eventually, however, the Romans were successful.

Marcellus, however, was no fool. He ceased further plans for frontal attacks on Syracuse. He decided instead to attack Syracuse from behind via land. With great

patience, Marcellus waited for his chance. His opportunity came while the Syracusans were celebrating a religious festival in honor of Artemis, the Greek goddess of the moon. The Syracusans ate and drank so much at their celebration that they forgot to keep a sharp lookout. Marcellus noticed that one section of the city wall had little protection. He seized his opportunity, attacking the surprised and drunken people of Syracuse. Marcellus captured the city.

MATHEMATICAL DEVOTION UNTIL THE END

When the Romans attacked, Archimedes was not celebrating with his fellow countrymen. Instead, he was quite involved trying to solve a problem. According to historians, Archimedes was a man capable of an intense amount of concentration. Often, when working on a problem, Archimedes concentrated so hard that he was oblivious to anything else going on around him.

Archimedes did not sleep when concentrating on a problem, and he often left meals untouched until he was finished with his work. Many times, Archimedes's servants had to drag him to his bath against his will so that they could bathe him and anoint him with oil. All the while, Archimedes would be drawing out geometrical figures on any surface he could find, including his own oil-slicked body. Archimedes's inattention to dress while working through a problem was demonstrated when he ran naked through the streets of Syracuse following his discovery of the law of buoyancy. If nothing else, these examples demonstrate his great passion for mathematics. Unfortunately, this passion may have cost him his life.

Upon taking the city, Marcellus sent soldiers immediately to find the mathematician responsible for the formidable weapons. The Roman general had great respect for Archimedes and ordered his troops not to harm him. Deeply engrossed in his work, Archimedes did not even know that Syracuse had fallen. He had not heard the shouting, the yells, or the blasting trumpets as the Romans swept through his city. He may not have even noticed the Roman soldier who approached him as he drew diagrams in the dirt.

In his biography of Marcellus, Plutarch relates some of the oral accounts on the death of Archimedes. In one

Although Marcellus ordered the capture of the great mind responsible for thwarting so many Roman attacks, he did not authorize Archimedes's death.

account, the soldier stepped on Archimedes's diagram. Incensed, the mathematician snapped, "Don't disturb my circles!" Another story states that Archimedes refused to obey the soldier's orders to accompany him to Marcellus until he had finished working out his problem. In any event, the Roman soldier was so enraged that he took out his sword and killed the seventy-five-year-old geometer.

Marcellus was deeply grieved when he heard of Archimedes's death. He ordered the execution of the soldier, stating that he was a common murderer. Marcellus also demanded of his troops that Archimedes be buried with honors. Marcellus commanded that Archimedes's friends and relatives be honored in the same way. He also made sure that, as Archimedes had wished, his tombstone bore the image of a sphere within a cylinder. This image represented his discovery that the volume of a sphere is two-thirds the volume of the smallest cylinder that encloses it, and that the surface of the sphere is also two-thirds the surface area of the cylinder. For example, a cylinder that contains a sphere filled with 4 gallons (15 liters) of water is able to hold 6 gallons (23 l) of water. Archimedes regarded this as his greatest discovery.

Archimedes had been proud of this achievement, and indeed, he should have been. To figure out that ratio today, a mathematician would use calculus, a very advanced form of mathematics, first discovered during the seventeenth century by Sir Isaac Newton and Gottfried Leibniz. However, Archimedes's technique so resembles calculus that perhaps he should share in some of this credit.

Following the death of Archimedes, mathematical progress came to a virtual standstill. His advancements in the field of mathematics made it nearly impossible for further progress to be made until new tools, such as algebra and analytical geometry, were developed. This would not happen until seventeen centuries later.

PICKING UP WHERE ARCHIMEDES LEFT OFF

Archimedes had hoped that his work would help those who followed him to discover more about mathematical relationships. However, in the decades following his death, Archimedes's influence was minimal. Historians suggest that this may have been due to the domination of the Roman Empire. The Greeks loved theoretical, abstract science, but the practical Romans had little interest in theoretical works, particularly mathematics. Only a few of Archimedes's ideas gained prominence—those that were relatively easy to understand and communicate. One such discovery was the approximate value of pi, which had become a standard mathematical notation during Roman times.

Following the defeat of Syracuse by Marcellus, the city became an outpost for the growing Roman Empire. Though the Romans had overtaken the city, they left Syracuse intact. The city fared far better than Carthage, which was destroyed by the Romans during the Third Punic War (149–146 BCE). In fact, Syracuse became the headquarters for the Roman government of Sicily and remained such for centuries to come.

Undoubtedly, Syracuse's governmental ties to Rome brought a lawyer and politician named Cicero to the city more than a century after Archimedes's death. While in Syracuse, Cicero searched for Archimedes's tomb and found it in a neglected state. Cicero wrote that the tomb was easy to identify because of its engraving of a sphere within a cylinder. In 75 BCE, Cicero had Archimedes's tomb restored. However, the tomb has since disappeared, and no one knows where Archimedes is buried now. Cicero also reported seeing a planetarium in Syracuse. According to Cicero, Archimedes built the planetarium, which showed the motion of the sun, the moon, and the five known planets. During Cicero's time, the planetarium was considered to be one of Archimedes's finest achievements. It was apparently made of spheres of glass and powered by water. It was so accurate that it could show the periods of the moon and predict the eclipses of the sun and moon.

For the most part, Archimedes's work was lost to the West for centuries. Much of the credit for Archimedes's rediscovery goes to a man named Regiomontanus, a Renaissance scientist who was a brilliant mathematician and a gifted linguist. Following the fall of Constantinople in 1453, many Greek-speaking people immigrated to the West, bringing with them ancient manuscripts. Regiomontanus understood the complicated mathematics found in the manuscripts, and he set out to translate them.

Starting in 1471, Regiomontanus began to mass-produce and mass-circulate the key Greek mathematical

Regiomontanus is credited with reviving Archimedes's discoveries. The Renaissance scientist translated and mass-produced Archimedes's manuscripts in the fifteenth century.

texts. Though killed by the plague that raged through Europe during the fifteenth century, Regiomontanus's assistant continued his work. In 1543, Nicolaus Copernicus used those very texts to develop his theory that the Earth revolves around the sun. During the mid-sixteenth century, some of Archimedes's more important works were published. The scientific community met them with immediate interest.

The works were translated into Italian, as well as in Latin, which was the language of the scientists. Archimedes's influence quickly spread through Italy and Europe and had an impact on some of the greatest minds known to mankind. Galileo was an Italian astronomer and physicist known for his study of motion. He was interested in things such as falling and rolling objects and projectiles. He took the next step in mechanics, picking up where Archimedes had left off centuries earlier.

THE METHOD

The rediscovery of Archimedes continues even into present day. One of his treatises, *The Method*, was found fairly recently, in 1906. While this work had been mentioned in other books, it was thought to be beyond rediscovery until a Danish scholar named J. L. Heiberg heard a report about a palimpsest that was located in the monastery of the Holy Sepulchre, in Jerusalem. A palimpsest is a parchment that has been written on more than once, with the original writing still being visible.

Upon examination of the document, Heiberg saw that it contained an Archimedean text. Apparently a monk living between the twelfth and fourteenth centuries had run out of paper for his prayer book. To remedy this, the monk took pages out of Archimedes's book, washed away the ink, turned them sideways, and wrote on them. Of course, in the past, when paper was not as plentiful as it is now, this was a common practice. Luckily, the monk had done a poor job of erasing Archimedes's writing. There was still a faint trace of Archimedes's text, most of which Heiberg was able to decipher. The underlying manuscript contained almost the entire text of the long-lost *The Method,* as well as versions of some of Archimedes's works that had already been rediscovered.

Finding *The Method* has been a key factor to our understanding of what led Archimedes to some of his discoveries. Perhaps there are more of his works out there, waiting to be found.

ARCHIMEDES'S LEGACY

Archimedes's work laid the foundation for modern mathematics. Though the details of some of the stories surrounding his life may be more legend than fact, his treatises and contributions made to both theoretical and applied mathematics cannot be denied. Archimedes discovered how to measure a circle, began the idea of developing a system for counting large numbers, and proved the laws of levers and pulleys. Archimedes also began the sciences of mechanics and hydrostatics, and he discovered the principles of buoyancy and specific gravity. With these, Archimedes set the world on a course that has led to the feats of science we have seen in recent years.

Even before his rediscovery, many scientists were already using Archimedes's works as their foundations. Though only nine of his treatises have been recovered, other scientists reference Archimedes in countless works. Among his lost papers were several addressing the subject of astronomy. This included one entitled "On Sphere-making," in which Archimedes described the construction of his planetarium.

Although he was considered a great astronomer during his time, Archimedes is not though of as an astronomer today. He was, however, probably a greater contributor to the field of astronomy than we will ever know. Because so many of his works have been lost, we will never know the true extent of Archimedes's influence.

Unlike most ancient mathematicians, Archimedes gained a reputation for his accomplishments in his own

Archimedes benefited from the knowledge of those who came before him, just as those who followed him owe the great mathematician and inventor a debt of gratitude.

time. However, the true genius of his work is probably appreciated more today than it was then. Today, we have the knowledge of all that was learned by those who came before us. In fact, the greatest scientific ideas of today are based upon things that other scientists learned in the past.

Sir Isaac Newton once said, "I could not have seen so far, had I not stood on the shoulders of giants." Archimedes had few giants on whose shoulders he could stand. He had only basic ideas and principles. However, Archimedes turned these into true, original scientific works of art. Galileo called him divine, saying that, without Archimedes, he could have achieved nothing. Archimedes was truly amazing. It is safe to say that when Newton spoke of "giants," he had Archimedes in mind.

TIMELINE

814 BCE Phoenician colonists establish the city of Carthage in northern Africa.

733 BCE Greek colonists from Corinth establish the city of Syracuse on the island of Sicily.

332 BCE Alexander the Great establishes the city of Alexandria in northern Egypt.

330 BCE Euclid is born.

300 BCE Ptolemy builds the museum in Alexandria.

323 BCE The Hellenistic period begins with the death of Alexander the Great.

306 BCE Hiero II, king of Syracuse, is born.

287 BCE Archimedes is born.

275 BCE Euclid dies.

CIRCA 270 BCE Hiero becomes king of Syracuse.

264 BCE The First Punic War begins.

263 BCE King Hiero signs a peace treaty with Rome.

247 BCE Hannibal, the Carthaginian general, is born.

241 BCE The First Punic War ends; Rome gains control of Sicily, except for Syracuse.

230 BCE Hiero's grandson Hieronymos is born.

218 BCE The Second Punic War begins.

215 BCE King Hiero dies; Hieronymos assumes the throne.

215 BCE Hieronymos switches allegiance from Rome to Carthage.

212 BCE Roman general Marcellus captures Syracuse.

212 BCE Archimedes is killed by a Roman soldier.

75 BCE Cicero discovers and restores Archimedes's tomb.

30 BCE The Hellenistic period ends with Rome's occupation of the last major Hellenistic kingdom.

30 BCE Vitruvius publishes an architecture book containing the story of Archimedes's discovery of the law of buoyancy.

75 CE Plutarch writes a biography about Marcellus that includes a biography of Archimedes.

1471 CE Regiomontanus begins mass-producing and mass-circulating Greek mathematical texts, including Archimedes's work.

1610 Ludolph van Ceulen calculates pi using a polygon with more than thirty billion sides.

1906 Archimedes's treatise *The Method* is discovered.

1981 Pi is calculated, with a computer, to more than two million decimal places.

1998 Archimedes's palimpsest containing *The Method* and Stomachion is sold at auction to an anonymous buyer.

1999–2008 The Walters Art Museum in Baltimore, Md., undertakes the process of conserving and studying the palimpsest.

GLOSSARY

APPLIED MATHEMATICS The branch of math concerned with using mathematics to solve questions that are outside of mathematics.

AREA The measurement of space within given parameters.

BUOYANCY The ability of a body or object to float in a fluid.

CIRCUMFERENCE The measurement of the outer boundary of a shape.

CONE A shape that tapers from a round bottom to a sharp point on top.

CYLINDER A round, elongated solid whose ends are circular.

CYNICISM An ancient Greek philosophy whose believers attempted to live a virtuous life in harmony with nature.

DENSITY The mass per unit volume.

DIALECT A form of language particular to a region.

DIMENSION A measurement in one direction in either space or time.

ELLIPSE A shape that resembles an elongated circle, one whose length is greater than its width.

EQUILIBRIUM Balance.

FORTIFICATION A fortress or protected area.

FULCRUM The point on which a lever is supported.

GEOMETRY A branch of mathematics that calculates shapes and their relationships to one another.

GRAVITY The force by which bodies are attracted to Earth's center.

HELLENISTIC Greek.

HUMANISM A philosophy that focuses on the needs and interests of people.

HYDRAULIC Relating to the movement of water or liquid.

HYDROSTATICS The scientific study of fluids at rest.

MUSE A poet.

NAVIGATOR The person who directs the ship's course.

PAPYRUS A tall, aquatic plant whose leaves the ancients often used as writing material.

PARABOLA A shape resembling that of a bowl.

SPECIFIC GRAVITY The ratio of a substance's density to the density of another substance that is used as a reference or standard.

SPHERE A shape that resembles a ball whose distance from the center to the surface is equal at all points.

SPIRAL A curve made by circling a fixed point, either by coming increasingly closer to it or by moving farther away from it.

STOICISM An ancient Greek philosophy that centers on the idea that life is predestined and that happiness results when people try to live their pre-planned lives.

THEORETICAL MATHEMATICS A branch of math concerned with abstract concepts. Also known as pure mathematics.

TREATISE A written document outlining a particular argument or position.

TYRANT A leader who controls everything.

VOLUME The space occupied by an object.

VORACIOUS Excessively eager.

FOR MORE INFORMATION

Arkimedion Museum

piazza Archimede

11 Palazzo Pupillo – Ortigia

96100 Syracusa, Sicily

Italy

This interactive museum is dedicated to the
  inventions of Archimedes. It is located in his
  hometown of Syracuse.

Bibliotheca Alexandrina

P.O. Box 138

Chatby 21526

Alexandria, Egypt

Website: http://www.bibalex.org

The New Bibliotheca Alexandrina, the New
  Library of Alexandria, is dedicated to recap-
  turing the spirit of openness and scholarship
  of the original Bibliotheca Alexandrina. It
  includes specialized libraries, museums, a planetarium, and research centers.

Drexel University

Drexel University Computer Science Department

Archimedes Home Page

3141 Chestnut Street

Philadelphia, PA 19104

(215) 895-2000

Website: http://www.mcs.drexel.edu/~crorres/
Archimedes/contents.html

A Drexel University professor has created this
information center about Archimedes, compil-
ing knowledge about Archimedes's inventions,
innovations, and works.

Mathematical Association of America

1529 18th Street NW

Washington, DC 20036-1358

(800) 741-9415

Website: http://www.maa.org

The Mathematical Association of America is a
member-driven organization, run by and for
members. Its mission is to advance the mathematical sciences, especially at the collegiate level.

Mathematical Sciences Research Institute

17 Gauss Way

Berkeley, CA 94720-5070

(510) 642-0143

Website: http://www.msri.org

The Mathematical Sciences Research Institute
(MSRI) is dedicated to the advancement and
communication of fundamental knowledge in
mathematics and the mathematical sciences,
to the development of human capital for the
growth and use of such knowledge, and to the
cultivation in the larger society of awareness
and appreciation of the beauty, power, and
importance of mathematical ideas and ways of
understanding the world.

PBS

NOVA/Infinite Secrets

1320 Braddock Place

Alexandria, VA 22314

Website: http://www.pbs.org/wgbh/nova/
archimedes

This companion website to NOVA's excellent
2003 program *Infinite Secrets* uses the Archimedes palimpset as a portal to Archimedes's
brilliant mind and great accomplishments.

The United Inventors Association of America

1025 Connecticut Avenue, Suite 1000

Washington, DC 20036

Website: http://www.uiausa.org

The United Inventors Association is a federally
registered nonprofit educational foundation
committed to providing educational resources
to the inventing community, while encouraging
honest and ethical business practices within the
industry service providers.

WEBSITES

Because of the changing nature of Internet links,
Rosen Publishing has developed an online list of
websites related to the subject of this book. This
site is updated regularly. Please use this link to
access this list:

http://www.rosenlinks.com/GGP/Arch

For Further Reading

Archimedes, with translation by Sir Thomas Heath. *The Works of Archimedes*. Mineola, NY: Dover Publications, 2013.

Asimov, Isaac. *Great Ideas of Science*. Boston, MA: Houghton Mifflin, 1969.

Bendick, Jeanne. *Archimedes and the Door of Science*. Warsaw, ND: Bethlehem Books, 1995.

Brooks, Philip. *Hannibal: Rome's Worst Nightmare*. New York, NY: Franklin Watts, 2009.

Charles River Editors. *Archimedes*. Charles River Editors, 2013.

Charles River Editors. *The Library of Alexandria*. CreateSpace Independent Publishing Platform, 2014.

Durant, Will. *The Story of Civilization*. New York, NY: Simon & Shuster, 1939.

Geymonat, Mario. *The Great Archimedes*. Waco, TX: Baylor University Press, 2011.

Gow, Mary. *Archimedes: Genius Mathematician*. New York, NY: Enslow, 2015.

Gow, Mary. *The Great Philosopher: Plato and His Pursuit of Knowledge*. New York, NY: Enslow, 2011.

Gow, Mary. *Measuring the Earth: Eratosthenes and His Celestial Geometry.* New York, NY: Enslow, 2010.

Graham, Amy. *Astonishing Ancient World Scientists and Great Brains.* New York, NY: Enslow Publishers, 2009.

Heath, Thomas. *Archimedes: Men of Science.* New York, NY: MacMillan, 1920.

Heath, Thomas L. *Greek Astronomy.* Mineola, NY: Dover Publications, 2011.

Hightower, Paul. *The Greatest Mathematician: Archimedes and His Eureka! Moment.* New York: Enslow Publishers, 2009.

Hirshfeld, Alan. *Eureka Man: The Life and Legacy of Archimedes.* New York, NY: Walker and Company, 2009.

Keyser, Paul T., and Georgia L. Irbiy-Massie, eds. *Encyclopedia of Ancient Natural Scientists.* New York, NY: Routledge, 2011.

Miles, Richard. *Carthage Must Be Destroyed.* New York, NY: Viking Press, 2011.

Netz, Reviel. *The Archimedes Codex.* Boston, MA: DeCapo Press, 2007.

Pollard, Justin. *The Rise and Fall of Alexandria: Birthplace of the Modern Mind.* New York, NY: Viking Press, 2006.

Reimer, Luetta, and Wilbert Reimer. *Mathematicians Are People, Too: Stories from the Lives of the Great Mathematicians.* Palo Atlo, CA: Dale Seymour Publications, 1990.

Soupious, M. A. *The Greeks Who Made Us Who We Are.* Jefferson, NC: McFarland, 2013.

Zannos, Susan. *The Life and Times of Archimedes.* Hockessin, DE: Mitchell Lane Publishers, Inc., 2005.

BIBLIOGRAPHY

Cajori, Florian. *A History of Mathematics.* New York, NY: Chelsea Publishing Co., 1991.

Heath, Sir Thomas. *History of Greek Mathematics.* New York, NY: Dover Publications, Inc., 1981.

Ipsen, D. C. *Archimedes: Greatest Scientist of the Ancient World.* Hillside, NJ: Enslow Publishers, Inc., 1988.

Muir, Jane. *Of Men & Numbers: The Story of the Great Mathematicians.* New York, NY: Dover Publications, Inc., 1996.

Toomer, Gerald J. "Archimedes." *The New Encyclopedia Britannica*, Vol. 13, 1988, pp. 930–931.

INDEX

ABOUT THE AUTHORS

Viola Jones is a teacher and writer who specializes in making U.S. history interesting to young adults.

Heather Elizabeth Hasan is a writer from Greencastle, Pennsylvania. She lives there with her husband, Omar, and their son, Samuel. Heather is fascinated by the early great thinkers who established the basis for much of what we know today. She would love to someday travel to places like Syracuse, Italy (Archimedes's birthplace) to see where it all began.

PHOTO CREDITS